Converging Paths

ALSO BY SUSAN SANTUCCI
Pathways to the Spirit

Converging Paths

*Lessons of Compassion, Tolerance, and Understanding
from East and West*

Susan Santucci

TUTTLE PUBLISHING
Boston • Rutland, Vermont • Tokyo

First published in 2003 by Tuttle Publishing, an imprint of Periplus Editions (HK) Ltd., with editorial offices at 153 Milk Street, Boston, Massachusetts 02109.

LC Card No.: 2002115843
ISBN: 0-8048-3476-8

Distributed by

North America, Latin America & Europe
Tuttle Publishing
Distribution Center
Airport Industrial Park
364 Innovation Drive
North Clarendon, VT 05759-9436
Tel: (802) 773-8930
Fax: (802) 773-6993
Email: info@tuttlepublishing.com

Japan
Tuttle Publishing
Yaekari Building, 3rd Floor
5-4-12 Osaki, Shinagawa-ku
Tokyo 141 0032
Tel: 81-35-437-0171
Fax: 81-35-437-0755
Email: tuttle-sales@gol.com

Asia Pacific
Berkeley Books Pte. Ltd.
130 Joo Seng Road
#06-01/03 Olivine Building
Singapore 368357
Tel: (65) 6280-1330
Fax: (65) 6280-6290
Email: inquiries@periplus.com.sg

First edition
06 05 04 03   10 9 8 7 6 5 4 3 2 1

Printed in Canada
Design by: Serena Fox Design

Dedication
For Michael and Justine

Acknowledgments

My sincerest thanks to my wonderful agent, Denise Shannon of ICM.
Her valuable feedback, support, and enthusiasm for this book were greatly
appreciated. Thank you to my friends and research assistants, Kathleen Ward,
Alex Ashline, Mary Guillemette, Jack Miller, and Karen Finnegan.
Thanks also to Eric Berke for his valued friendship and great coaching.
My appreciation to Beth Greenberg for taking such good care of Sam.
A very special thanks to Andrew Szanton for his editing and invaluable support.
I am very grateful to have him as a friend and mentor.
My deepest thanks to my splendid editor, Ed Walters, for
championing this project at Tuttle.
Thank you, also, to Helen Watt at Tuttle for her feedback on the final manuscript.
Finally, I'd like to thank my mother, Mary Chernov, for her artwork.

Table of Contents

Introduction, 11

The Law of Abundance, 14
Know the Divine Value of Your Life, 16
Believe, 18
Know That You Are Never Alone, 20
Go on a Spiritual Retreat, 22
Recognize the Power of Words, 24
Follow Your Bliss, 26
Work at What You Enjoy, 28
Seek Spiritual Friendship, 30
Find Community, 32
Embrace Suffering, 34
Practice Compassion, 36

Love without Fear, 38

Transform Anger, 40

Draw Strength from Your Troubles, 42

Never Give Up Hope, 44

Cultivate Resiliency, 46

Learn Acceptance, 48

Contemplate Eternity, 50

Give Faith Time to Take Root, 52

Love, 54

Seek True Abundance, 56

Learn to Accept the Flaws of Others, 58

Serve Others, 60

Practice Kindness, 62

Seek True Strength, 64

Know That God Works through Others, 66

Release Your Worry, 68

Love Laughter, 70

Live in This Moment, 72

Celebrate Daily Miracles, 74

Attend to Your Spirit, 76

Patience in Adversity, 78

Transform Despair, 80

See the Kingdom of Heaven, 82

Practice Gratitude, 84

Pray from the Heart, 86

Pray for Your Enemies, 88

See the Sacred in Daily Life, 90

Look for the Good in People, 92

Dwell in the Light, 94

Savor Silence, 96

Live and Let Live, 98

The Secret to Success, 100

Take Action, 102

The Art of Happiness, 104

The God Within, 106

The Law of Attraction, 108

Watch for Saints, 110

Realize the Power of Purpose, 112

Recognize the Power of Thought, 114

Respect All Religions, 116

Trust in the Divine Plan for Your Life, 118

Keep Good Company, 120

Practice Forgiveness, 122

Grow Spiritually, 124

Persevere, 126

Transform Your Suffering, 128

Accept Change, 130

Value a Person's Actions, Not His Words, 132

Know That Love Will Survive Death, 134

Courage, 136

Humility, 138

True Love, 140

Impermanence, 142

The Purpose of Life, 144

The Importance of a Smile, 146
Understanding Breeds Compassion, 148
Plant and Nurture Seeds of Joy, 150
Cultivate Mindfulness, 152

Bibliography, 154
Credits, 158

Introduction

*We have to allow what is good, beautiful, and
meaningful in the other's tradition to transform us.*
—*Thich Nhat Hanh*

Over the past decade, thousands of Americans have been creating
highly personal forms of worship, drawing ideas from different faiths
and teachers. Studies show that baby boomers and Generation Xers are
five times more likely than their parents to search outside the religion of
their childhood for spiritual answers. They want a religion that speaks
directly to their personal lives, keeps pace with the changes in modern
society, and gives a personal experience of the divine. Many are nourished by more than one spiritual root, have more than one guide, or even
belong to two distinct religions. Americans have been turning in record
numbers to the East to nourish their spiritual lives. Buddhism is now one
of the fastest-growing faiths in America.

The East has a great deal to offer. But what is it? The East has developed,
over 3,500 years, some of the best methods for attaining God awareness
found anywhere in the world. The East also offers centuries of wisdom on
the art of happiness and concrete ways to deal with stress and anxiety.

Introduction

You may be surprised to find out how smoothly Eastern practice can complement, and even strengthen, your own spirituality or religious faith. Eastern faiths let us see our own religion with new eyes. My own spiritual search is an example. I was raised a Christian, but I never truly embraced the teachings of Jesus until I found Buddhist and Swami teachers who embodied Christ's love and compassion. Take, for example, the Eastern view of suffering. We all know the Western approach to suffering is influenced by the commercial culture we live in. Take an aspirin. Buy a sports car. Buy off your pain. But Buddhism teaches that life is inseparable from suffering. Devout Buddhists ask, "How can we embrace suffering?" Western thought is adept at making apt distinctions between things. It's no surprise that many Western thinkers have defined such things as God, heaven, and divinity as things apart from us. But Eastern mystics see no separation between the worldly and the divine. This view may take some getting used to. But it offers an amazing vision for westerners who seek a direct experience of the sacred.

Although there are differences in emphasis, at their core, the teachings of great saints are very similar. The original teachings of Jesus and Buddha share themes of kindness, compassion, love, tolerance, and passion for individual awakening. They took different routes to the same destination. People who have God awareness don't quibble over the narrow differences between traditions. They recognize one another as brothers. As Gandhi said, "God has no religion."

Introduction

Balancing values from both traditions may be the greatest key to happiness and fulfillment. Buddhist Zen master Thich Nhat Hanh said, "To me religious life is life. I do not see any reason to spend one's whole life tasting just one kind of fruit. We can be nourished by the best values from many traditions."

Converging Paths is an inspirational collection of parallel sayings from great Eastern and Western teachers. From Jesus and Buddha to Mother Teresa and the Dalai Lama, these words can inspire, inform, and nourish your spirit. Each page offers a pair of dynamic quotes, followed by a practical piece of advice, written to offer comfort, guidance, hope, and encouragement.

This little book is thought provoking but fun. It will challenge you to expand your outlook. Whatever your faith, these timeless thoughts can recharge your being. Lose yourself in these pages—they will offer your spirit the greatest wisdom of the ages. Even a few moments of practice, done fully, can alter the rest of your day.

—*Susan Santucci*
Cambridge, Massachusetts

The Law of Abundance

What goes out from you
comes back to you again.

—*Mencius*
4th c. B.C. Chinese philosopher

Give and it will be given to you.
—*Luke 6:38, NRSV*

Goodness and happiness exist in abundance. You can create them through your generosity.

Know the Divine Value of Your Life

I wish I could be like Asita and Simeon,
the holy men who came to see the Buddha and Jesus,
and tell you how important your birth is.

—Thich Nhat Hanh

That is why I say unto you,
"For your sakes I came down."
You are the beloved.

—Epistle of John 4:16, KJV

Jesus said that in the great scheme of things, you will find that your life is one single day and your sufferings one single hour. So awake to how brief and precious your life really is. Cherish each day.

Believe

Since our thoughts and words are the seeds that will bring forth
our harvest of the future, I will begin today
to fill my consciousness with the ideas of abundance.

—*Paramahansa Yogananda*

In the center of your own soul
choose what you want to become, to accomplish . . .
Every day in the silence of absolute conviction know that
it is now done. . . . Imagine yourself to be what you want to be.
See only that which you desire, refuse even to think of the other.
Stick to it, never doubt.
Say many times a day, "I am that thing."

—*Ernest Holmes*

Replace negative thoughts
with positive ones.
Act as if you believe,
and in time your belief
will take root.

Know That You Are Never Alone

I am always with all beings;
I abandon no one.
And however great your inner darkness,
you are never separate from me.

—*The Bhagavad Gita*

Lo, I am with you always,
even unto the end of the world.

—*Matthew* 28:20, *KJV*

Just as the wave is never separate

from the mighty ocean,

so our soul is never separate

from God.

Go on a Spiritual Retreat

Every person needs a retreat, a "dynamo" of silence,
where he may go for the exclusive purpose of being newly
recharged by the Infinite.

—*Paramahansa Yogananda*

If you do not fast from the world,
you will not find the Father's kingdom.
If you do not observe the sabbath
as a sabbath, you will not see the Father.

—*The Gospel of St. Thomas* 27:1-2

Once a year, take time for a spiritual retreat. Withdraw from the stress and chaos of life. Recharging your spirit can give you a whole new perspective on life.

Recognize the Power of Words

A team of fast horses cannot overtake a word
once it has left the lips.

—Ancient Chinese saying

For what goes into your mouth will not defile you,
but that which issues from your mouth—
it is that which will defile you.

—The Gospel of St. Thomas 14:5

Watch what you say,
for words have the power
to heal or to
destroy.

Follow Your Bliss

Let yourself be silently drawn
by the strange pull of what you really love.
It will not lead you astray.

—*Rumi*
13th c. Sufi master

I say follow your bliss and don't be afraid,
and doors will open where you didn't know
they were going to be.

—*Joseph Campbell*

Follow your intuitions
of where your bliss is.
Pursue your inner inclinations
and unfinished dreams.

Work at What You Enjoy

If you choose a job that you like,
you will never have to work a day in your life.

—*Confucius*

Blessed is he who has found his work.

—*Thomas Carlyle*
19th c. British author

The surest way to find happiness

is to work at what you enjoy.

If you have not yet found such work,

search passionately for it.

You will be best at work you love.

Seek Spiritual Friendship

Just as the dawn is the forerunner of the arising of the sun,
so true friendship is the forerunner of the arising
of the noble eightfold path.

—*The Buddha*

For those who dwell in the world and desire
to embrace true virtue, it is necessary to unite themselves
together by a holy and sacred friendship.
By this means they encourage, assist, and conduct
one another to good deeds.

—*St. Francis de Sales*

Encourage and inspire your friends. Make dinner for a friend in times of struggle, heartbreak, or distress. Offer deep compassion or honest advice. Rejoice in a friend's good fortune. Take them out to celebrate a promotion or an engagement.

Find Community

The family stands together like a forest,
while storms blow down the tree that stands alone.

—Jataka 74
Buddhist sacred scripture

To be rooted is perhaps the most important
and least recognized need of the human soul.

—Simone Weil

Without human connection,
we perish. Even strong communities
have their failings.
Find the best spiritual group
you can and savor its jewels
and wisdom. Take what you need
and leave the rest.

Embrace Suffering

Unless we agree to suffer,
we cannot be free from suffering.

—D. T. Suzuki

The chief pang of most trials is not so much the actual
suffering itself as our own spirit of resistance to it.

—Jean Nicolas Grou
18th c. Christian mystic

Our resistance to suffering
is what causes us the worst pain.
The first step to freeing ourselves
from suffering is to admit our
suffering, to acknowledge the
depth of our pain,
and to embrace this pain.

Practice Compassion

The ocean of tears cannot drown us
if compassion is there.

—Thich Nhat Hanh

God's compassion is fathomless,
refreshing the soul . . .
sweeter than honey from the comb.

—Psalm 19

The great saints are overflowing
with compassion. Emulate them.
Show compassion to those
around you. Your compassion
is not complete if it does not
include yourself.

Love without Fear

When love beckons to you,
follow him,
Though his ways
are hard and steep.
And when his wings enfold you,
yield to him,
Though the sword hidden among
his pinions may wound you.

—*Kahlil Gibran*

There is no fear in love; but perfect love casteth out fear.

—*I John 4:18, KJV*

When we fear love, what we really
fear is losing love or being hurt.
Ask yourself, "What would I do if I
knew I couldn't fail?"
Now do it.
Cast off fear.

Transform Anger

You will not be punished for your anger,
you will be punished by your anger . . .
Let a man overcome anger by love.

—*The Buddha*

For every minute you are angry,
you lose sixty seconds of happiness.

—*Ralph Waldo Emerson*

Giving in to anger

leads you further from the Divine.

Draw Strength from Your Troubles

Any disturbance in our lives ought to be viewed as a test of God,
meant to instruct and strengthen us.
A chain is only as strong as its weakest link;
each one of us is only as strong as our greatest weakness.
We must learn to stand calm, unshaken, undismayed,
no matter what comes in life.

—*Daya Ma*
President, Self-Realization Fellowship

God allows us to experience the low points of life
in order to teach us lessons we could learn in no other way.

—*C. S. Lewis*

View your problems as teachers.

What lessons do they have for you?

Never Give Up Hope

When your bow is broken and your last arrow spent,
then shoot, shoot with your whole heart.

—*Zen saying*

Even if our efforts of attention seem for years to be
producing no result, one day a light that is in exact
proportion to them will flood the soul.

—*Simone Weil*

Never stop pursuing your dreams.
Even when it looks darkest,
your persistence will be rewarded.

Cultivate Resiliency

Our greatest glory is not in never failing,
but in rising every time we fall.

—*Confucius*

I can't go on.
You must go on.
I'll go on.

—*Samuel Beckett*

*When we see a person
survive tragedy, we are witnessing
the sustaining power
of the Divine, a spark of the
divinity within.*

Learn Acceptance

Accept everything that arises. Accept your feelings,
even the ones you wish you did not have.
Accept your experiences, even the ones you hate.
Don't condemn yourself for having human flaws and failings.
Learn to see all the phenomena in the mind as being perfectly
natural and understandable.
Try to exercise a disinterested acceptance at all times
with respect to everything you experience.

—*Bhante Henepola Gunaratana*

When I accept others as they are, they change.
When I accept myself as I am, I change.

—*Carl Rogers*

Acceptance appears easy,
but it is not. True acceptance gives
us freedom from suffering.
Only when you accept your
feelings can you begin
to transform them.

Contemplate Eternity

When one sees Eternity in things that pass away
and Infinity in finite things,
then one has pure knowledge.

—*The Bhagavad Gita*

To see a world in a grain of sand,
And heaven in a wild flower,
Hold infinity in the palm of your hand,
And eternity in an hour.

—*William Blake*

To catch a glimpse of eternity,
look at things that are small and
transient—but look with a keen and
loving eye, and a wild, kind heart.

Give Faith Time to Take Root

Act as if you had faith and in time
faith will take hold of you.

—*Sufi saying*

Trust in the Lord with all thine heart.

—*Proverbs* 3:5

Your heart may be troubled.

That's no matter.

Lay down your burden.

Let faith take root.

Love

The Buddha is born of love, patience,
gentleness, and truth.

—*Vimalakirti, Nirdesha Sutra 2*

When the evening of life comes,
we shall be judged on love.

—*St. John of the Cross*

Happiness is determined not by how much you have accomplished but by how much you have loved.

Seek True Abundance

No fault is greater than the desire to acquire.
For, to know that enough is enough
is to have always enough.

—*Tao Te Ching*

Desire only that which has already been given.
Want what you already have.

—*Rabran Gamliel*
15th c. Hebrew scholar

Practice gratitude.

Real abundance comes when we see

the possessions of others without

jealousy. Focus on the abundance

in your life. Let jealousy wither.

Learn to Accept the Flaws of Others

Seek not every quality in one individual.

—*Confucius*

Here is a mental treatment guaranteed to cure every ill
that flesh is heir to: sit for half an hour every night
and mentally forgive everyone against whom
you have any ill or antipathy.

—*Charles Fillmore*
Cofounder of New Thought movement

Judge others with compassion.

Accept their flaws,

for without compassion for others

we can find no love and

compassion for ourselves.

Serve Others

The more we take the welfare of others to heart and work for their
benefit, the more benefit we derive for ourselves.
This is a fact that we can see.

—*The Dalai Lama*

It is one of the most beautiful compensations
of this life that no man can sincerely try to help
another without helping himself.

—*Ralph Waldo Emerson*

When you do a favor for someone,

you create a sweet human

connection between you.

The more you give to others,

the more you will receive.

Practice Kindness

People ask me what is my religion.
I tell them, "My religion is kindness."

—*The Dalai Lama*

Kindness has converted more people than zeal,
science or eloquence.

—*Mother Teresa*

Kindness is utterly profound,
a kind of worship that converts
those it touches.

Seek True Strength

A tree that is unbending
is easily broken.

—*Lao Tzu*

One must learn to sail in all winds.

—*Italian proverb*

Flexibility is a sign of strength.
The bamboo tree is both
the fastest-growing tree on earth
and the strongest.

Know That God Works through Others

My firm belief is that He reveals Himself daily
to every human being, but we shut our ears to the
"still small voice." We shut our eyes to
the "pillar of fire" in front of us.

—*Mahatma Gandhi*

God Himself does not speak prose, but
communicates with us by hints, [signs],
inferences and . . . objects lying all around us.

—*Ralph Waldo Emerson*

Divine love is the source

behind human love.

Divine love is there every day

for us to see—

if we will only see it.

Release Your Worry

Worry is usually a fear that something
undesirable is going to happen
that hardly ever does.

—*Paramahansa Yogananda*

My life has been filled with terrible misfortunes,
most of which have never happened.

—*Mark Twain*

Never worry alone.
Talk out your problems with others.
Release your worry by fixing on
something or someone new.

Love Laughter

Time spent laughing
is time spent with the gods.

—*Japanese proverb*

We shall never know all the good
that a simple smile can do.

—*Mother Teresa*

Laughter is medicine for the soul.
Laughter takes us outside ourselves.
It puts our problems in perspective.
Reserve time for people who make
you laugh. Never go an entire day
without a good laugh.

Live in This Moment

The past should not be followed after, the future not desired.
What is past is got rid of, and the future has not come.
But whoever has vision now here,
. . . of a present thing . . . let him cultivate it.
Swelter at the task this very day.
Who knows whether he will die tomorrow?
There is no bargaining with
the great hosts of Death.

—*The Buddha*

We must not wish anything other than what happens
from moment to moment.

—*St. Catherine of Genoa*

God works in moments.

Pay attention to this very moment.

It is full of treasures

for the patient.

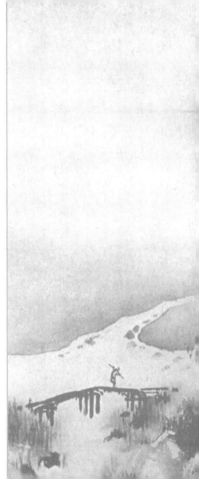

Celebrate Daily Miracles

People usually consider walking on water
or in thin air a miracle.
But I think the real miracle is not to walk either on water
or in thin air, but to walk on earth.
Every day we are engaged in a miracle which we don't even
recognize: a blue sky, white clouds,
green leaves, the black, curious eyes of a child—
our own two eyes. All is a miracle.

—*Thich Nhat Hanh*

Where there is great love, there are always miracles.
—*Willa Cather*

Miracles are God's calling card,

engraved invitations to belief.

Attend to Your Spirit

Know that this body is like a garment.
Go, seek the wearer of the garment, do not lick (kiss)
the garment . . .You are such that without the material body
you have a spiritual body: do not, then,
dread the going forth of the soul from the body.

—*Rumi*

Among my patients in the second half of life—
that is to say over thirty-five—there has not been one
whose problem in the last resort was not that of finding a
religious outlook on life. None of them had been really healed
who did not regain this religious outlook.

—*Carl Jung*

As you grow older,
your body may fail
but not your spirit.
Treat your body with respect,
but live in the spirit.

Patience in Adversity

Behind every adversity
lies a hidden possibility.

—*Sufi saying*

There is no education
like adversity.

—*Benjamin Disraeli*

Believe deeply in your own success.

Failure is a part of the journey.

Know that failure often brings you

one step closer to success.

Adversity makes success so much

sweeter when success comes.

Transform Despair

Even loss and betrayal
can bring us awakening.

—*Jack Kornfield*

God often gives in one brief moment that
which he has for a long time denied.

—*Thomas à Kempis*

Life runs in cycles.
The wheel never stops turning.
No matter how dark the night,
morning comes. No matter how cold
the winter, spring comes. When you
feel despair, know that the wheel is
turning. Joy will come.

See the Kingdom of Heaven

Each step you make should bring you
into the Pure Land of the Buddha.

—*Thich Nhat Hanh*

It will not come by watching for it.
It will not be said, "Look, here!" or "Look, there!"
Rather, the Father's kingdom is spread out upon the earth,
and people don't see it.

—*The Gospel of St. Thomas 113:1-4*

Find a spiritual teacher who can begin to show you how to walk in the kingdom of heaven even while you are alive. Walk alone, and with others, along sacred paths that are well worn, and down paths that are brand new.

Practice Gratitude

A thankful person is thankful under all circumstances.
A complaining soul complains even if he
lives in paradise.

—Bahá'u'lláh
Founder of Bahá'i faith

If thank you is the only prayer you say,
that will be enough.

—Meister Eckhart
14th c. Christian Mystic

Gratitude lets you see the gifts and
abundance that are already
in your life.
Start a gratitude journal.
Each day write down five things
for which you are grateful.

Pray from the Heart

Worship me through meditation
in the sanctuary of the heart.

—*Srimad Bhagavatan*
Indian Vedic text

The secret of success in prayer is to be simple,
direct, and spontaneous.

—*Emmet Fox*
20th c. New Thought author

Pray from your heart.
Heartfelt prayers work best.
God answers all prayers—
sometimes in unexpected ways.

Pray for Your Enemies

For hate is not conquered by hate:
hate is conquered by love.
This is eternal law.

—*The Buddha*

Love your enemies, do good to those who hate you,
bless those who curse you,
pray for those who abuse you.

—*Luke 6:27, KJV*

Make no enemies.
Use your antagonists to give
yourself practice in tolerance.
Pray for the person
you are angry with.
It is impossible to be angry
at someone and to pray for him
at the same time.

See the Sacred in Daily Life

Zen is not some kind of excitement,
but concentration on our usual
everyday routine.

—*Shunryu Suzuki*

Remember, remember the sacredness of things
running streams and dwellings
the young within the nest
a hearth for sacred fire
the holy flame.

—*Omaha Indian tribe chant*

Wherever you dwell with awareness

—that is sacred ground.

Look for the Good in People

No one can ever gain strength
by brooding over his weakness.
—*Paramananda*
20th c. Indian saint

Treat people as if they were what they ought to be,
and you help them to become
what they are capable of being.

—*Johann Wolfgang von Goethe*

Look for goodness and the divine

presence in everyone you meet.

Focus on what they are doing right.

When you want to change yourself,

focus on what you, too,

are doing right.

Dwell in the Light

There are two ways of passing from this world—
one in light and one in darkness.
When one passes in light, he does not come back;
but when one passes in darkness,
he returns.

—*The Bhagavad Gita*

Jesus spoke unto them, saying, "I am the light of the world.
Whoever follows me will never walk in darkness
but will have the light of life."

—*John* 8:12, *KJV*

Nurture your inner light. Spend time with the people and things that bring you joy. When you touch joy, you touch the Divine. Light is a common metaphor for God or Spirit. The Quakers speak of cultivating the "inner light"—the spark of divinity in each of us. Quakers say that there is that of God in every person.

Savor Silence

Silence is the language of God:
it is also the language of the heart.

—*Swami Sivanda*

Let us be silent that we may hear
the whispers of the gods.

—*Ralph Waldo Emerson*

Commune with God

through silent meditation.

Live and Let Live

As far as possible, one should not interfere
in the affairs of others.

—*Sri Ramana Maharshi*

He who would be serene and pure
needs but one thing, detachment.

—*Meister Eckhart*

When your loved ones are troubled,

help them body and soul.

But at some point, to protect your

own soul, be prepared to detach

yourself from them.

Do this with care and with love,

but with firmness, too.

The Secret to Success

Doubt not;
when you want to attain any righteous goal,
cast away the thought of failure.
As you are a child of God,
believe that you have access to all things
that belong to Him.

—*Paramahansa Yogananda*

No thought of discouragement or disorder should ever be created,
but only positive assurance, strong thoughts of success . . .
the feeling that with God all things are possible,
the belief that we are One with that Great Mind.
These are the thoughts that make for success.

—*Ernest Holmes*

The best secret to success
is to believe that you will succeed.
Remember that successful people
do the hard things that nobody else
wants to do.

Take Action

Call on God, but row for the shore.

—Indian proverb

Do not be too timid and squeamish about your actions.
All life is an experiment.
The more experiments you make the better.
What if they are a little coarse, and you may get your coat
soiled or torn? What if you do fail, and get fairly rolled
in the dirt once or twice?
Up again; you shall never be so afraid of a tumble.

—Ralph Waldo Emerson

Don't wait until you feel
motivated to start a project.
Motivation comes after action.
Appeal to God, but don't wait for
His divine solace.
Act.

The Art of Happiness

If you want others to be happy, practice compassion.
If you want to be happy, practice compassion.

—*The Dalai Lama*

The art of being happy
lies in the power of extracting happiness
from common things.

—*Henry Ward Beecher*

Do something simple that you love to do—right now. Don't dwell on regrets about the past or fears of the future. Live in the present, and plan for the future. Defer the profound things to a later time or to an easier time.

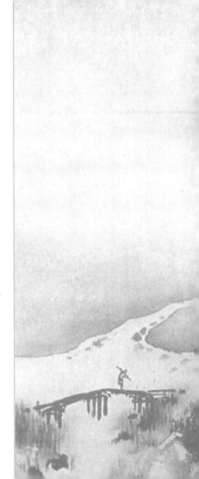

The God Within

God's light is contained in the heart of each.

—*Arjan*
5th guru of Sikhism

I was wandering like a lost sheep,
searching outside of myself for that which was within.
I ran through all the streets and squares of this great city,
the world, searching for Thee, O God, and I found Thee not,
because I sought Thee wrongly.
Thou wert within me and I sought Thee without.

—*St. Augustine*

Take a few minutes each day to commune with the God within. The greatest journey is within ourselves. Don't be distracted by material things outside yourself. Don't be tempted by the cold glory of the crowded city. Dwell in the warm house of your own soul.

The Law of Attraction

Thanksgiving and praise open in your consciousness
the way for spiritual growth and supply to come to you.
Spirit pushes Itself out into visible manifestation as soon as
a channel is opened through which It can flow.

—*Paramahansa Yogananda*

A good practice is to sit and realize that you are
a center of Divine attraction, that all things are coming to you,
that the power within is going out and drawing back all that you
will ever need . . . . Declare that you are now in the midst of
plenty . . . those who believe the most always get the most.

—*Ernest Holmes*

To create more abundance,
rid your mind of all thoughts
of failure. Affirm that you are now
open, ready to receive the good
that is now yours.

Watch for Saints

To encounter a true master is worth a century
of studying his or her teaching.
How can we encounter a true master? It depends on us.
Many who looked directly into the eyes of the Buddha
or the eyes of Jesus
were not capable of seeing them.

—*Thich Nhat Hanh*

You read the face of the sky and of the earth,
but you have not recognized the one who is before you,
and you do not know how to read this moment.

—*The Gospel of St. Thomas* 91:2

Stay on the lookout for God.
What is subtle is easily missed.
As Jesus said, "There will be days
when you will look for me
and will not find me."

Realize the Power of Purpose

Happiness comes when your work and words
are of benefit to others.

—*Jack Kornfield*

Happiness is obtained through fidelity
to a worthy purpose.

—*Helen Keller*

Write a mission statement
for your life. Read it each week
and plan your day with it in mind.
You may notice little difference
at first. But over time,
this humble practice
will transform your life.

Recognize the Power of Thought

What we are today comes from our thoughts
of yesterday, and our present thoughts build our life of tomorrow:
our life is the creation of the mind.

—*The Buddha*

One single stream of thought, daily sent out into Creative Mind
[God], will do wonders. Within a year the person
who will practice this will have completely changed
his conditions of life. The way to practice this is daily
to spend some time in thinking and in mentally seeing
just what is wanted; see that thing just as it is wished and then
affirm that this is now done.

—*Ernest Holmes*

Our thoughts create our life.
Be attentive to your own thoughts.
Whatever you believe and focus on,
you will manifest.

Respect All Religions

Don't hang on exclusively to any particular creed so that you
disbelieve the rest, or you will disregard much that is good and
miss the real Truth. Allah is omnipotent and omnipresent and is
not contained by any one religion, for he says in the Qur'an
"Wherever you turn, there is the face of Allah."

—*Ibn Arabi*

I believe that by openness to Buddhism, to Hinduism,
and to these great Asian traditions, we stand a wonderful chance
of learning more about the potentiality of our own traditions . . . .
The combination of the natural techniques and the graces . . .
that have been manifested in Asia and the Christian liberty of the
gospel should bring us all at last to that full and transcendent
liberty which is beyond mere cultural differences and mere externals.

—*Thomas Merton*

See the good in other religions.
Scrutinize them for what can enrich
your own practice.

Trust in the Divine Plan for Your Life

What then is man's duty?
What else can it be? It is just to take refuge in God and to pray to
Him with a yearning heart for His vision.

—*Sri Ramakrishna*

True peace consists in not separating ourselves
from the will of God.

—*St. Thomas Aquinas*

A divine plan is working

in your life.

Use the prayer,

"Thy will, not mine, be done."

Keep Good Company

If we keep "wise company," as the Buddha said,
and have good friends, we have one of the greatest resources
for happiness and freedom.

—*Sharon Salzberg*

If you have enough love, you'll be the happiest
and most powerful person in the world.

—*Emmet Fox*

Good company is a great blessing.
Seek out the people in whose presence
you feel uplifted and esteemed.
Spend time with them. Choose your
closest friends, business associates,
and life companion with the utmost
care, for they will hugely
influence your happiness.

Practice Forgiveness

Where there is forgiveness
there is God himself.

—*Kabir*
15th c. Indian religious poet

If we could read the secret history of our enemies
we should find in each man's life sorrow and suffering
enough to disarm all hostility.

—*Henry Wadsworth Longfellow*

Pray for the person

who hurts you.

Grow Spiritually

Therefore we know that, unawakened,
even a Buddha is a sentient being,
and that even a sentient being,
if he is awakened in an instant of thought,
is a Buddha.

—*Hui Neng*
6th patriarch of Zen Buddhism

In Zen enlightenment, the discovery of the
"original face before you were born" is the discovery
not that one sees Buddha but that one is Buddha.

—*Thomas Merton*

The seed of enlightenment is in you,

waiting to be watered.

Persevere

The hardest things in the world begin with what is easy;
the greatest things in the world begin
with what is minute. Therefore, the saint
never does anything great
and so is able to achieve the great.

—*Tao Te Ching*

Nothing great was ever done
without much enduring.

—*Catherine of Siena*

Don't lose sight of your goal.

Work toward it every day,

a little at a time.

Transform Your Suffering

I teach one thing and one thing only:
that is, suffering and the end of suffering.

—*The Buddha*

Life is difficult.
This is the great truth, one of the greatest truths.
It is a great truth because once we see this truth,
we transcend it.

—*M. Scott Peck*

The Buddha taught that the First Noble Truth is that "Life is suffering." When we embrace our suffering, accept it, and look deeply into it, we can discover the root cause of our suffering and take right action to reduce our suffering. Thus, embracing suffering, looking deeply into it, is the first step to transcending suffering.

Accept Change

When the way comes to an end,
then change—
having changed you pass through.

—*I Ching*
Chinese sacred text

Every exit is an entry somewhere else.

—*Tom Stoppard*

Life is a series of changes.
The sooner you learn to embrace
change, the happier you'll be.
Change brings fear of the unknown.
Embrace your fear, go deeply into it,
observe its nuances,
and fear will recede.

Value a Person's Actions, Not His Words

To carry out an enterprise in words is easy;
to accomplish it by acts
is the sole test of man's capacity.

—*Ramayana*
Indian sacred text

It is in our lives and not our words
that our religion must be read.

—*Thomas Jefferson*

Love is shown not by words

but by sweet deeds.

Know That Love Will Survive Death

Every good work which thou art able to do today,
do not postpone for tomorrow . . . for there have been many
people whose remaining life was one day, and they have been
taken away in the presence of fifty years' work.

—*Sad Dar* 81:10-12
16th c. Zoroastrian scripture

It is good to have a reminder of death before us,
for it helps us to understand the impermanence of life
on this earth, and this understanding may aid us
in preparing for our own death.
He who is well prepared is he who knows
that he is nothing compared with Wakan-Tanka,
who is everything;
then he knows that world which is real.

—*Black Elk*

Know that love will survive death.
Savor the time you spend
with loved ones. You can never tell
them "I love you" too often.
Death lets us see deeply that the
nature of life is impermanence and
shows us the sacredness of life
in each moment.

Courage

Courage is fear that has said its prayers.

—*Author unknown*

Whatever you do, you need courage.
Whatever course you decide upon,
there is always someone to tell you you are wrong.
There are always difficulties arising,
which tempt you to believe that your critics are right.
To map out a course of action
and follow it to an end, requires . . . courage.

—*Ralph Waldo Emerson*

Confucius said that courage is the

greatest of all the virtues—

because it makes all the

other virtues possible.

Humility

Be humble and you will remain entire.
The sage does not display himself, therefore he shines.
He does not approve himself, therefore he is noted.
He does not praise himself, therefore he has merit.
He does not glorify himself, therefore he excels.

—*Tao Te Ching*

Should you ask me:
what is the first thing in religion?
I should reply: the first, second, and third thing
therein is humility.

—*St. Augustine*

Humility enables us to move toward others and to find our proper place in the scheme of things.

True Love

We really have to understand the person we want to love.
If our love is only a will to possess, it is not love.
If we only think of ourselves, if we know only our own needs
and ignore the needs of the other person,
we cannot love. We must look deeply in order to see
and understand the needs, aspirations, and suffering
of the person we love. This is the ground of real love.
You cannot resist loving another person
when you really understand him or her.

—*Thich Nhat Hanh*

The beginning of love is to let those we love
be perfectly themselves,
and not to twist them to fit our own image.
Otherwise, we love only the reflection of
ourselves we find in them.

—*Thomas Merton*

To truly love, we must be willing to really listen. Ask your loved one, "Dear one, what can I do to bring you more joy today?"

Impermanence

All is transient.
When one sees this, he is above sorrow.

—*The Buddha*

There is nothing permanent except change.

—*Heraclitus*

6th c. B.C. Greek philosopher

The third noble truth
discovered by the Buddha
is the truth of impermanence.
The moment you see just how
impermanent everything in life is,
every sunset, every meal,
every loved one, the more you
cherish each day.

The Purpose of Life

The soul is here for its own joy.

—*Rumi*

The goal of life is rapture.

—*Joseph Campbell*

Discover your rapture and you will resonate in your innermost being. Your rapture is what gives you a flow experience, a feeling of being so absorbed in an activity that you lose all sense of time and feel only exhilaration.

The Importance of a Smile

The smile is a very important feature of the human face.
But because of human intelligence, even the good part of human
nature can be used in the wrong way, such as sarcastic smiles or
diplomatic smiles, which only serve to create suspicion.
I feel that a genuine, affectionate smile largely depends on one's
attitude. It is illogical to expect smiles from others if one does not
smile oneself. Therefore, one can see that many things
depend on one's own behavior.

—*The Dalai Lama*

Let us make one point, that we meet each other with a smile,
when it is difficult to smile. Smile at each other,
make time for each other in your family.

—*Mother Teresa*

Practice smiling. Smile and greet

someone new every day.

Learn to draw people to you

with smiles.

Understanding Breeds Compassion

If we practice looking deeply into [our enemy's] situation and the causes of how he came to be the way he is now, and if we visualize ourselves as being born in his condition, we may see that we could have become exactly like him. When we do that, compassion arises in us naturally, and we see that the other person is to be helped and not punished. In that moment, our anger transforms itself into the energy of compassion.

—*Thich Nhat Hanh*

Don't criticize another man until you have walked a mile in his moccasins.

—*Native American proverb*

Jesus said, "With all thy getting,

get understanding."

True understanding

leads to compassion.

Plant and Nurture Seeds of Joy

Why cling to the pain and the wrongs of yesterday?
Why hold on to the very things that keep you
from hope and joy?

—*The Buddha*

Profound joy of the heart is like a magnet
that indicates the path of life.
One has to follow it,
even though one enters into a way full of difficulties.

—*Mother Teresa*

Pay close attention to the activities

and people you most enjoy.

When you feel pure joy, you are

very close to the Divine presence.

Cultivate Mindfulness

And further, a monk knows when he is going, "I am going."
He knows when he is standing, "I am standing."
He knows when he is sitting, "I am sitting."
He knows when he is lying down, "I am lying down."

—*The Buddha*

If you see things as they are here and now,
you have seen everything that has happened from all eternity.
All things are an interrelated Oneness.

—*Marcus Aurelius*

Mindfulness is the quality
of presence in the moment.
It allows us to see the nature of things.
Mindfulness helps us to be
with what truly matters.

BIBLIOGRAPHY

Augustine, Saint. *The Confessions of St. Augustine*. New York: P. F. Collier & Son Company, 1909.

Barks, Coleman, trans. *The Essential Rumi*. San Francisco, California: HarperSanFrancisco, 1994.

Beckett, Samuel. *Three Novels by Samuel Beckett: Molloy, Malone Dies, and The Unnamable*. New York: Grove Press, 1995.

The Bhagavad Gita. Translated by Swami Nikhilananda. New York: Ramakrishna-Vivekananda Center, 1944.

Bhagavatan, Srimad. *The Wisdom of God*. Hollywood, California: Vedanta Press & New York: Putnam's & Sons, 1943.

Blake, William. *The Complete Poetry and Prose of William Blake*. New York: Anchor, 1982.

Campbell, Joseph and Bill Moyers. *The Power of Myth*. New York: Doubleday, 1988.

Champion and Short. *Readings from World Religions*. Boston: Beacon Press, 1951.

The Chinese Classics. Translated by James Legge. Worcester, Massachusetts: Z. Baker, 1866.

Covey, Stephen. *The 7 Habits of Highly Effective People*. New York: Simon & Schuster Inc., 1989.

Dalai Lama. *The Art of Happiness: A Handbook for Living*. New York: Riverhead, 1998.

————. *A Simple Path*. London, England: Thorsons, 2000.

Das, Bhagavan. *Essential Unity of All Religions*. Bombay, India: Bharatiya Vidya Bhavan, 1960.

The Dhammapada. Translated by Juan Mascaro. New York: Penguin Books, 1973.

Emerson, Ralph Waldo. *Poetry and Imagination*, 1876.

BIBLIOGRAPHY

Fillmore, Charles. *Teach Us to Pray*. Unity Village, Missouri: Unity, 1997.

The Five Gospels. Translated by Robert Funk, Roy Hoover, and the Jesus Seminar. San Francisco, California: HarperCollins, 1993.

Gandhi, Mahatma. *Ghandi Speaks*. Los Angeles, California: Self-Realization Fellowship.

Gibran, Kahlil. *The Prophet*. Herts, United Kingdom: Wordsworth Editions Ltd., 1997.

Goddard, Dwight. *A Buddhist Bible*. Boston: Beacon Press, 1970.

Gunaratana, Henepola. *Mindfulness in Plain English*. Boston: Wisdom Publications, 1993.

Hanh, Thich Nhat. *Be Still and Know*. New York: Riverhead, 1996.

—————. *Peace Is Every Step*. New York: Bantam, 1991.

—————. *The Miracle of Mindfulness*. Boston: Beacon Press, 1999.

—————. *Living Buddha, Living Christ*. New York: Riverhead, 1997.

Holmes, Ernest. *Creative Mind and Success*. New York: R. M. McBride & Company, 1919.

The Holy Bible. King James Version.

The Holy Bible. Revised Standard Version.

The Holy Bible. New Revised Standard Version.

James, William. *The Varieties of Religious Experience*. New York: Penguin Books, 1982.

BIBLIOGRAPHY

Keller, Helen. *Helen Keller's Journal*, 1936–37. New York: The American Foundation for the Blind.

Kornfield, Jack. *Buddha's Little Instruction Book*. New York: Bantam Books, 1994.

Krishnamurti, J. *Total Freedom*. San Francisco, California: HarperCollins, 1996.

Longfellow, Henry Wadsworth. *Driftwood*, 1857.

Lyall, L.A. *Mencius*. London: Longmans Green, 1932.

Merton, Thomas. *Thoughts in Solitude*. New York: Noonday Press, 1956.

Mitchell, Stephen. *Tao Te Ching: A New English Version*. Harper Perennial, 1992.

Muller, Max. *Sacred Books of the East*. Oxford: Clarendon Press, 1887.

Peter, Laurence. *Peter's Quotations*. New York: Bantam Books, 1977.

Rilke, Ranier Maria. *Poems*. Translated by Jessie Lemont. New York: Columbia University Press, 1943.

Rogers, Carl. *A Way of Being*. New York: Mariner Books, 1995.

Salzberg, Sharon. *Lovingkindness*. Boston: Shambhala Publications, 1995.

Suzuki, D. T. *Zen Buddhism: Selected Writings of D. T. Suzuki*. New York: Doubleday, 1996.

Suzuki, Shunryu. *Zen Mind, Beginner's Mind*. New York: Weatherhill, 1997.

BIBLIOGRAPHY

Tao Te Ching: The Wisdom of Lao Tzu. Translated by Jacob Trapp. Sante Fe, New Mexico: Jacob Trapp Publisher.

Templeton, John Marks and James Ellison. *Riches for the Mind and Spirit*. San Francisco, California: HarperCollins, 1990.

Mother Teresa. *A Simple Path*. New York: Ballantine Books, 1995.

Tolle, Eckhart. *The Power of Now: A Guide to Spiritual Enlightenment*. Novato, California: New World Library, 1999.

Weil, Simone. *The Need for Roots: Prelude to a Declaration of Duties Toward Mankind*. Florence, Kentucky: Routledge Inc., 1949.

Woods, Ralph. *The World Treasury of Religious Quotations*. New York: Hawthorn Books, 1966.

Yogananda, Paramahansa. *The Divine Romance*. Los Angeles: Self-Realization Fellowship, 1986.

CREDITS

Barks, Coleman, trans. *The Essential Rumi*. San Francisco, California: HarperSanFrancisco, 1994.

Campbell, Joseph and Bill Moyers. *The Power of Myth*. Copyright ©1988 by Apostrophe S Productions, Inc., and Bill Moyers and Alfred van der Marck Editions, Inc. for itself and the estate of Joseph Campbell. Used by permission of Doubleday, a division of Bantam Doubleday Dell Publishing Group, Inc.

Hanh, Thich Nhat. *Be Still and Know*. Copyright © 1996 by Thich Nhat Hanh. Reprinted with permission of Riverhead Books, a division of Penguin Putnam.

———. *Living Buddha, Living Christ*. Copyright © 1995 by Thich Nhat Hanh. Reprinted with permission of Riverhead Books, a division of Penguin Putnam.

———. *The Miracle of Mindfulness*. Copyright ©1975 by Thich Nhat Hanh. Used by permission of Beacon Press.

———. *Peace is Every Step*. Copyright ©1991 by Thich Nhat Hanh. Used by permission of Bantam Books, a division of Bantam Doubleday Dell Publishing Group, Inc.

Kornfield, Jack. *Buddha's Little Instruction Book*. Copyright ©1994 by Jack Kornfield. Used by permission of Bantam Books, a division of Bantam Doubleday Dell Publishing Group, Inc.

Salzberg, Sharon. *Lovingkindness*. Copyright ©1995 by Sharon Salzberg. Used by permission of Shambhala Publications.

CREDITS

Sri Daya Mata. Quotations from the writings of Sri Daya Mata published by Self-Realization Fellowship, Los Angeles. Used by permission of Self-Realization Fellowship.

Suzuki, D. T. *Zen Buddhism: Selected Writings of D. T. Suzuki.* Copyright ©1996 by D. T. Suzuki. Used by permission of Doubleday, 1996.

Yogananda, Paramahansa. Quotations from the writings of Paramahansa Yogananda published by Self-Realization Fellowship, Los Angeles. Used by permission of Self-Realization Fellowship.

ABOUT THE AUTHOR

Susan Santucci is a teacher and writer on spirituality.
She holds a degree from Amherst College and a
master's degree in education from Harvard
University. She lives in Providence, Rhode Island.